MARTIAL ARTS IN ACTION

CAPOEIRA

MARTIAL ARTS IN ACTION

# CAPOEIRA

BY JOHANNAH HANEY

Marshall Cavendish
Benchmark
New York

Other Marshall Cavendish Offices:
Marshall Cavendish International (Asia) Private Limited, 1 New Industrial Road, Singapore
536196 • Marshall Cavendish International (Thailand) Co Ltd. 253 Asoke, 12th Flr, Sukhumvit
21 Road, Klongtoey Nua, Wattana, Bangkok 10110, Thailand • Marshall Cavendish (Malaysia)
Sdn Bhd, Times Subang, Lot 46, Subang Hi-Tech Industrial Park, Batu Tiga, 40000 Shah Alam,
Selangor Darul Ehsan, Malaysia

Marshall Cavendish is a trademark of Times Publishing Limited

All websites were available and accurate when this book was sent to press.

Library of Congress Cataloging-in-Publication Data

Haney, Johannah.
Capoeira / Johannah Haney.
p. cm. — (Martial arts in action)
Includes index.
ISBN 978-0-7614-4932-4 (print)
ISBN 978-1-60870-362-3 (ebook)
1. Capoeira (Dance)—Juvenile literature. I. Title.
GV1796.C145H36 2012
793.3'1981—dc22
2010013829

Editor: Peter Mavrikis
Publisher: Michelle Bisson
Art Director: Anahid Hamparian
Series design by Kristen Branch

Photo research by Candlepants Incorporated

Cover Photo: ©ArenaPal / Topham / The Image Works

The photographs in this book are used by permission and through the courtesy of:
*Alamy Images*: © John Warburton-Lee Photography, 2, 17; © David Mena Arrastia, 6; © Stefano Paterna, 8;
© Hemis, 9; © Matt Fagg RF, 10; © Vittorio Sciosia, 16; © Ruby, 19; © Image Source RF, 26; © PhotoStock-
Israel, 28; © JoeFox, 29; © Paul Paris, 32; © CuboImages srl, 36, 23; © Harriet Cummings, 24. *The Image
Works*: ©ArenaPal / Topham, 12, 31, 34; © Jeff Greenberg, 22. *Art Archive*: Private Collection / Marc
Charmet, 14. *University of Virginia*: "jogar capoera ou danse de la guerre"; Image Reference NW0171,
as shown on www.slaveryimages.org,. sponsored by the Virginia Foundation for the Humanities and the
University of Virginia Library, 15. *Getty Images*: Ryan McVay, 21; Christopher Pillitz, 38; Bongarts/Getty
Images for DFB, 39; SambaPhoto/Angelo Pastorello, 41; Deborah Jaffe, 43; 42.

Printed in Malaysia (T)
1 3 5 6 4 2

# CONTENTS

# CHAPTER ONE
# CAPOEIRISTAS

**A** GROUP OF PEOPLE STAND IN A CIRCLE, playing musical instruments, singing, and clapping to the rhythm of music. Two people from the circle move to the middle. They crouch low to the ground, arms in front of their faces, and begin shifting back and forth in a fluid motion. One person kicks a leg high in the air while the other gracefully moves to a low, crouched position in order to avoid the kick. They move in rhythm to music the others in the circle are playing. Each movement is like water, graceful and smooth. Yet it is clear their movements are powerful.

The people in this circle are practicing or playing capoeira, a form of martial arts from Brazil. Capoeira is a martial art, but it is more than that. It is also a game, a dance, and a cultural tradition. People who practice capoeira are known as **capoeiristas**.

**CAPOEIRA MUSICIANS PLAY MUSIC TO SET THE RHYTHM FOR THE GAME.**

THE CIRCLE OF CAPOEIRA—KNOWN AS THE RODA—IS MADE UP OF MEMBERS WHO SING, PLAY MUSIC, AND CLAP.

## CAPOEIRA: A DANCE, A MARTIAL ART, A GAME

The movements of capoeira are synchronized, or matched in time, between players. Because of that and the dancelike movements often used, capoeira is considered a kind of dance. But it is also a fighting technique that uses **sweeps**, **feints**, and kicks. However, most people who practice capoeira do not make physical contact with their opponents. Capoeira is also a game. The two people who are playing capoeira are opponents. Yet in capoeira, there is no clear-cut winner or loser, and no scoring system.

Capoeira is a unique form of martial arts that combines playing music, dancing, and acrobatics. Capoeiristas form a circle, known as a *roda*. The circle form keeps the energy of the game focused. Within the circle, the *jogo*, or game, is played. Two players come forward and begin the jogo within the circle. Players rotate between

A JOGO BEGINS WITH TWO CAPOEIRISTAS FROM THE RODA.

CAPOEIRISTAS CAN BE MEN OR WOMEN, BOYS OR GIRLS.

being part of the roda and coming forward to start a new jogo. Each do their best in the roda and learn from each other as they play.

## MEET A CAPOEIRISTA

John is a twelve-year-old living in California. He recently started learning how to do capoeira. Once a week, he goes to a roda at his local YMCA, where capoeiristas of many different skill levels—male and female, kids of all ages and even some adults—meet to play. John is just learning the basic moves of capoeira, but he can be part of the roda even with players who are more advanced than he is. He can use even the most basic movements to have a meaningful game. As he plays with students at his level, at a more advanced level, and even at a lower level, he learns important lessons about capoeira. John is also learning the music of capoeira and many words in the Portuguese language. Practicing capoeira is helping him to gain strength and flexibility. The pleasure he gets as he learns and perfects new moves makes him feel good about himself and his skills. For John, capoeira is improving his health and his **self-confidence**.

# CHAPTER TWO
# THE HISTORY OF CAPOEIRA: THE BRAZILIAN SLAVE DANCE

**C**APOEIRA BEGAN IN BRAZIL. The exact origins are not known, but many believe that slaves brought from Africa to Brazil during the 1500s developed capoeira. Slave owners did not want slaves to fight and exercise, because they could be injured, and it wasted time. Capoeira was most likely developed to hide fight moves. By making attacks look like a dance, slaves could fight one another and exercise without the slave owners realizing it.

Another theory about where capoeira comes from suggests that it developed from a traditional dance called *N'golo*. The N'golo, or "dance of the zebras," was a dance that warriors performed in a ceremony that celebrated a girl's initiation to womanhood. Some people believe that N'golo and capoeira are the same. Others think

**THIS CAPOEIRISTA PLAYS THE BERIMBAU, A STRINGED INSTRUMENT THAT SERVES AS THE BASIS OF MOST CAPOEIRA MUSIC.**

THIS ENGRAVING FROM THE MID-NINETEENTH CENTURY SHOWS SLAVES DANCING ON A SLAVE SHIP. CAPOEIRA IS BELIEVED TO HAVE ROOTS IN THE SLAVES OF BRAZIL, AND SOME BELIEVE ITS ORIGINS BEGIN IN AFRICA.

that N'golo was similar to capoeira, but both developed separately from Afro-Brazilian roots.

In 1888, the slaves in Brazil were freed. Newly freed slaves practiced capoeira in the streets of Brazil. But in 1892, a law made it illegal to practice capoeira. If someone were a capoeirista, they were considered a criminal. However, the law did not stop capoeiristas from forming rodas in private and in the streets. Capoeira was finally made legal again in the 1930s. Around this time, the image of capoeira began to change. Important academies began teaching the art of capoeira. It was at this time that two separate forms of capoeira emerged.

THIS IMAGE, CALLED CAPOEIRA OR THE DANCE OF WAR, WAS DONE BY JOHANN MORITZ RUGENDAS, A GERMAN PAINTER, IN 1825.

## TWO FORMS OF CAPOEIRA

There are two main styles of capoeira: capoeira Angola and capoeira regional. These two styles represent the different ways that capoeira developed in different regions of Brazil.

### CAPOEIRA ANGOLA

Capoeira Angola is thought to be the more traditional form of this martial art. Capoeira Angola is generally slower and more playful, but with a focus on precision, or getting the moves just right. Vincente Ferreira Pastinha, commonly known simply as Mestre Pastinha, is known as the father of capoeira Angola. Mestre Pastinha learned capoeira when he was a young boy. He was often pushed around by a big bully. An African man named Benedito recognized that Pastinha was being bullied by other children, and took Pastinha aside to show him some capoeira movements to defend himself.

As an adult, Mestre Pastinha taught capoeira at the Centro Esportivo de Capoeira Angola—a capoeira academy in Salvador, a city on the northeast coast of Brazil. He taught many students and his academy became famous for traditional capoeira.

THIS CAPOEIRISTA IS PRACTICING A SWEEP WHILE HIS OPPONENT DODGES THE KICK.

# Mestre Bimba

Manuel dos Reis Machado, commonly known by his nickname Bimba, is considered the father of capoeira regional. He was born in 1900 in Salvador, Brazil, and began learning capoeira when he was twelve years old. At this time, practicing capoeira was illegal in Brazil. Mestre Bimba is credited with helping to end the ban against capoeira. In 1928 he performed at the palace of the Governor of Bahia (in the city of Salvador). The governor was impressed, and in the 1930s capoeira was made legal in Brazil once again. Mestre Bimba opened one of the first schools to teach capoeira, Academia-escola de Cultura Regional. He performed for the president of Brazil, Getúlio Dorneles Vargas, after which he was granted permission to teach capoeira. Mestre Bimba helped transform the image of capoeira from a criminal activity to something to be respected and admired.

THE HISTORIC OLD CITY OF SALVADOR IS THE HOME OF MESTRE BIMBA, AND THE BIRTHPLACE OF CAPOEIRA REGIONAL.

## CAPOEIRA REGIONAL

Capoeira regional is more fast-paced and emphasizes the fighting and acrobatics of capoeira. The father of capoeira regional is considered to be Manuel dos Reis Machado, often known simply as Mestre Bimba. Mestre Bimba began learning capoeira when he was twelve. But within a few years, he began adding movements from *batuque*, a Brazilian fighting form that focused on sudden attacks. This transformed capoeira regional into a more fighting-focused form. Mestre Bimba was a very popular and successful teacher, and his new style of capoeira spread far and wide.

Today, many people practice both forms of capoeira throughout the world. Some people specialize in either capoeira Angola or capoeira regional. Others practice a combination of both styles, sometimes adding new techniques that do not come from either capoeira regional or capoeira Angola. This style is known as capoeira contemporânea. Many people believe that in order to have the fullest command of capoeira, a student should study both forms. Usually a student will start learning capoeira in one of the styles, and gradually begin to learn more about the other style as he or she progresses.

## THE MUSIC OF CAPOEIRA

The people who make up the circle play instruments, sing, and clap. The music sets the pace and tone of the jogo. Slower rhythms will result in a slower jogo. There are several musical instruments that are needed in a roda. One is called the **berimbau**. The berimbau's sound resonates from a *cabaça,* a gourd that is hollow. The gourd is attached to the bottom of a long, curved wooden bow about 4 feet

THE BERIMBAU IS THE CENTRAL INSTRUMENT OF THE RODA. THESE COLORFUL GOURDS THAT ARE THE BASE OF THE BERIMBAU ARE CALLED CABAÇAS.

(a little over 1 meter) long. This bow is known as a *verga*. A steel wire called an *arame* is strung to either end of the bow. To play the berimbau, a stick called a *baqueta* is struck against the steel wire. A small stone or coin is held against the steel wire at different times to change the way it sounds. Some musicians hold a **caxixí** in their hand as well. A caxixí is a small woven basket that contains seeds for a rattling percussion sound.

There are three different kinds of berimbaus, each with a different tone. The *gunga* is a berimbau that plays the lowest tones. The capoeirista playing the gunga is usually the leader of the roda. He or she will lead the singing, and often calls players into the game. The berimbau called the *médio* has a medium tone. The *viola* has the highest tone of all the berimbaus. A roda will have between one and three berimbau players at one time.

Other musicians in the roda play a variety of percussion instruments. One is the *pandeiro*. The pandeiro is a hand-held drum with a round wooden frame and six pairs of cymbals on the outside. It is similar to a tambourine, however the pandeiro can be tuned to create a different tones, and the cymbals have a more crisp sound than those on a tambourine. Pandeiro players use a variety of techniques to make percussion sounds with a range of different notes and sounds. The pandeiro is considered Brazil's national instrument, and is often used in samba music.

*Agogô* is another instrument that is sometimes present in the roda. It is a set of metal bells of different sizes that are struck with a stick. The agogô makes a high-pitched, clear sound.

# TOQUES— THE RHYTHM OF THE RODA

The music played by the roda sets the tone for the game played by the capoeiristas. The toques are the rhythms played in a song of capoeira. Players know what kind of game to play based on the toque that is being played by the members of the roda. The mestre sets the toque for each game of capoeira. The Angola toque is a slower rhythm, and tells players that the movements should be closer to the ground. This is one of the most traditional toques in capoeira. The Iuna is another toque, but this one is very fast and leads to a lively game with a lot of acrobatic movements. São Bente Grande has a medium-paced rhythm, and indicates that the game is played with a standing stance.

THE BERIMBAU PLAYER USUALLY SETS THE RHYTHM, OR TOQUE, FOR THE JOGO.

MUSIC IS AN INTEGRAL PART OF THE RODA OF CAPOEIRA.

The main rhythm in a capoeira roda comes from the *atabaque*. Atabaques are large wooden drums with a system of ropes on the outside. Around the top edge of the drum there is a metal rim, which is under the ropes. There are wooden wedges between this metal rim and the body of the drum. When a player hammers on the wooden wedges, the ropes get tighter. Other times the rope may be looser. This changes the sound of the drum and can raise or lower the tones the drum makes. Players use their hands to drum, using different techniques to achieve different types of sound. For example, hitting the drum with a cupped palm creates a more hollow sound, while

THIS CAPOEIRISTA PLAYS THE ATABAQUE.

ABADÁS ALLOW CAPOEIRISTAS TO MOVE FREELY THROUGHOUT THE ACROBATIC MOVEMENTS OF THE JOGO.

hitting the drum flat on its edge produces a sharp sound.

Many songs played in the roda have lyrics, or words, sometimes in English, often in Portuguese, and sometimes a mix of both languages. In some songs, the leader of the roda sings a line and the other members of the roda repeat the line. This style of singing is known as call and response. The lyrics often talk about the culture, history, and philosophy of capoeira.

## PHILOSOPHIES OF CAPOEIRA

Capoeiristas have a strong connection to the history and cultural heritage of the game. The roots of capoeira are an important part of playing the game. The lyrics of capoeira songs celebrate Brazil and the development of capoeira.

One important philosophy of capoeira is the circle of the roda. The shape of the roda is important to capoeira. The energy that is created by the music and the game are kept inside the circle. Each person who makes up the circle is a vital part of the roda. Without each person, the circle would be broken. Members of the roda play music, sing, and clap during a game of capoeira. In this way, each person in the circle is involved in the game.

Another philosophy of capoeira is that a person does not become a master capoeirista overnight. In fact, it is considered to be a life-long process of continued learning and growth. The longer a person plays capoeira, the more the person learns about the martial art and about life.

# CHAPTER THREE

# PART OF THE RODA

A STUDENT WHO IS BEGINNING TO LEARN CAPOEIRA will start with the most basic movement in capoeira, the *ginga*, which is a rocking movement. He or she will also begin to learn about the history and philosophy of capoeira, as well as the music. Once a student knows the basics, he or she can start to play capoeira.

## THE RANKING SYSTEM

Capoeira does not have a standardized ranking system as many other martial arts do. However, there is a similar progression among different types of capoeira. The system of ranking is sometimes called the cordas, and may involve different colored cords that indicate rank. The levels of study are *aluno* (student), *graduado* (graduate), *formado* (formed), *professor* (teacher), and *mestre* (master).

**THIS DEMONSTRATION OF A CAPOEIRA MOVE DISPLAYS THE AGILITY REQUIRED TO PERFORM MORE ADVANCED CAPOEIRA MOVEMENTS.**

A TYPICAL CAPOEIRA CLASS WILL FOCUS ON LEARNING SPECIFIC MANEUVERS THAT MAKE UP THE MARTIAL ART.

Capoeira Angola does not use any belt or cord system. Students move from one level to another based on the student's progress as observed by his or her teacher. For example, once an aluno has mastered the basic techniques and has learned the history and some language, his or her mestre might advance that student's level to graduado.

THIS YELLOW CORDA OF CAPOEIRA REGIONAL INDICATES A BEGINNER STUDENT.

Capoeira regional, however, does use a more formal system of cords to rate the level of advancement of its students. Different groups use different colors for the cords that are given as students achieve the next level. There is no universal set of guidelines to dictate when a student of capoeira should move on to the next level. Instead, it is up to the teacher to determine when a student has improved. In capoeira regional, ceremonies to introduce new students and to give students new cords are called **batizados e troca de cordas**, which literally means, baptism and changing of cords.

## CAPOEIRA MOVEMENTS

Capoeiristas can spend a lifetime mastering all the movements and techniques that make up this unique combination of martial art and dance. Students usually first learn a few basic movements on which more advanced movements are based.

### GINGA

This is the movement upon which capoeira is based. With feet shoulder-width apart, capoeiristas move their feet in a rocking motion, placing one foot behind the other with knees bent, then returning the foot to the original position and repeating with the other foot.

During the movement of the lower body, the capoeirista alternates placing each forearm in front of the head. The ginga makes the motions of the capoeirista fluid and continuous. It helps set the timing and rhythm of the dance. It also confuses other capoeiristas about what movements might come next.

## AÚ

The **aú** is the capoeira version of a cartwheel. Often the arms and legs are bent during the cartwheel. Sometimes during an aú, the player stops upside down in order to perform a type of hand stand. The capoeirista may also sweep the legs in an arc in order to kick the opponent.

PERFORMING THE MOVEMENTS OF CAPOEIRA WELL REQUIRES AWARENESS OF EACH PART OF THE BODY.

THE YOUNG CAPOEIRISTA ON THE RIGHT DODGES A KICK.

## ESQUIVA

Esquiva actually means "to escape." With one leg bent, the capoeirista bends at the waist over the bent leg in order to dodge a kick. There are several types of esquiva movements, depending on which angle is being used for escape. *Esquiva de frente* is a very low dodge. *Esquiva al lado* is a side dodge. *Esquiva diagonal* is a dodge that also helps move the player forward.

## NEGATIVA

In *negativa norma*, the capoeirista drops low to the ground, with one leg bent close to the chest and one leg extended. The body is

# Capoeira for Everyone

Capoeira is an intense physical activity. Capoeiristas with physical challenges of many types come together to learn and play capoeira. Mestres have trained capoeiristas with missing limbs, artificial limbs, and in wheelchairs. Because capoeira involves a wide range of different types of movement, capoeiristas with a wide range of physical challenges can be part of the roda. Players who are blind or deaf can join the roda and celebrate the tradition of capoeira. Other mestres are training people with Down syndrome. Mestre Pastinha, considered the father of capoeira Angola, summed up the inclusiveness of this martial art: "Capoeira is for men, women, and children; the only ones who don't learn it are those who don't wish to."

CAPOEIRA IS A PHYSICALLY INTENSE MARTIAL ART. HOWEVER IT ALSO INCORPORATES PHILOSOPHY, MUSIC, HISTORY, AND CULTURE.

supported with one arm. The other arm is protecting the face. This movement can be used to avoid an attack or to start an attack. Other forms of negative include *negative lateral,* in which the body is extended in a sideways position low to the ground. *Negative derruband* has the body stretched sideways with one leg extended forward.

## ROLÊ

This movement is one of a few ways to move across distance in the capoeira roda. From a low stance, the player spins to one side, spinning in a full circle. It can be combined with many other moves. The key to a successful rolê is to always keep an eye on the opponent. While the back is to the opponent during the spin, a capoeirista can look under the legs to see what is going on behind him or her.

## DRESSING FOR THE RODA

There is no universal uniform for people who play capoeira. However, many schools provide a uniform that includes pants called **abadás**. Abadás are pants that fit snugly at the waist, but are usually wide-legged to allow for a wide range of movements. Many types of abadás have loops around the waist for students to wear their cordas. Many capoeira schools require a certain type of abadás that has the logo of the school printed on the left hip. Some schools allow students to train wearing whatever clothing they choose, and reserve the uniform for more formal demonstrations. Other schools do not require a uniform at all. At these schools, capoeiristas wear comfortable clothing that is easy to move in.

# CAPOEIRA AND YOU

L IKE ANY SPORT, THE BEST WAY to learn is to be instructed by a professional. Capoeira has some great acrobatic movements that should only be performed with experience and under the proper supervision. Capoeira classes and programs can be found in many places. A local martial arts studio, a gym, or the YMCA often have classes in capoeira. Many mestres also have their own capoeira schools, open for anybody who wants to learn.

When you find a capoeira program, do not feel that you have to join that one. See if you can sit in on a few classes to see how they are taught. If you feel comfortable with the teachers and other students, you may want to give it a try. If the class seems too advanced or if you would prefer to learn different styles, do not hesitate to look elsewhere. Feeling comfortable in a learning environment is essential to practicing a martial art.

STUDENTS OF ANY AGE CAN BEGIN LEARNING CAPOEIRA. THIS
YOUNG GIRL IS JUST BEGINNING HER TRAINING.

MEMBERS OF THE RODA CAN BE VARIOUS AGES AND LEVELS OF SKILL AND STILL PLAY A MEANINGFUL GAME TOGETHER.

## IMPROVING PHYSICAL AGILITY AND HEALTH

Practicing capoeira requires strength, flexibility, and balance. When a person does capoeira, his or her muscles get stronger. Flexibility allows a person to move more freely and helps prevent injury. Playing capoeira is a rigorous activity. It requires **stamina**, which is the ability to maintain a high level of energy for an extended length of time. Most capoeiristas also have good reflexes. The art has helped them to train their bodies to respond quickly to movements, motions, and actions.

Capoeira also provides **cardiovascular exercise**. Cardiovascular exercise helps keep the heart and lungs healthy and strong. Experts believe that every person should get some form of cardiovascular exercise that is appropriate to their age, weight, and lifestyle. Along with proper diet and other exercises, the physical activities of capoeira can help a person achieve and maintain a healthy weight.

## CULTURE, LANGUAGE, AND HISTORY

Many people first become interested in a martial art because they want to learn more about a foreign culture or the history of a region. Capoeira is an excellent way to learn some things about the Brazilian and Afro-Brazilian culture.

CAPOEIRA IS PLAYED THROUGHOUT THE WORLD. THIS DEMONSTRATION IS BEING PERFORMED IN GERMANY.

Learning capoeira is not just about understanding how to move the body. The culturally rich history of capoeira also provides a link to the past. In order to advance in capoeira, a student must learn about the history and culture behind the art. The lyrics in many capoeira songs teach important history lessons about the roots of capoeira and important mestres.

The music of capoeira can also enrich the lives and minds of capoeiristas. In order to play the music of the roda, many learn to play one of the instruments. Those who do not play an instrument still sing, clap, and participate in the music.

Learning capoeira also means learning many words in Portuguese. The words used in capoeira are all words from Brazilian Portuguese. When capoeiristas sing songs in the roda in Portuguese, they begin to learn more vocabulary and more about the language. People who play capoeira throughout their lives end up knowing a lot of Portuguese words. Many go on to learn how to speak the language in order to communicate with capoeiristas around the world.

## LIFE SKILLS

Capoeira can have many other benefits that are more difficult to measure, but have a very positive effect. Capoeira helps students develop discipline. Following directions, knowing how to behave, and when to back off are important parts of capoeira instruction. Working with other students and teachers in the roda improves social skills and the ability to cooperate. This builds teamwork. To be a successful capoeirista, a person must have respect for his or her opponent. Self-respect can also develop from practicing capoeira.

A YOUNG BOY IN BRAZIL PRACTICES CAPOEIRA MOVEMENTS IN THE STREETS OF HIS HOMETOWN.

# CAPOEIRA IN
# U.S. CULTURE

ACTOR WESLEY SNIPES, A TRAINED CAPOEIRISTA, USES MOVEMENTS INSPIRED BY CAPOEIRA IN SOME OF HIS FILMS.

Capoeira may be a centuries-old martial art from Africa by way of Brazil, but it has become part of the cultural landscape in the United States in recent years. Today, capoeira is integrated in many areas of U.S. culture, from movies to video games, modern dance to music. The screen actor Wesley Snipes often uses capoeira movements in his action films, as he is a trained capoeirista.

The 2004 action film *Ocean's Twelve* featured some capoeira movements. Musicians including the members of Soulfly, Ben Harper, and others have used berimbau in their compositions. The band Black Eyed Peas used capoeira movements in the music video for the song *Mas Que Nada*, which they recorded with Brazilian singer Sérgio Mendes. The critically-acclaimed dance troupe Pilobolus uses capoeira movements in their choreography. Capoeira even appears in advertising. The car company Mazda uses a capoeira song in one of their television ads: *Zum Zum Zum*.

CAPOEIRA CAN IMPROVE PHYSICAL FITNESS, MENTAL FOCUS, AND MUSICAL ABILITY.

As a student improves and moves up the ranks, he or she can feel good about those accomplishments. Those good feelings can often extend to other parts of a student's life—to schoolwork, friendships, and other relationships. Capoeira helps to build confidence and self-esteem.

With its intriguing moves and numerous benefits, it is no wonder that capoeira is a very popular martial art. Capoeiristas are graceful and powerful fighters and dancers. But they are also an important part of continuing the legacy of the roda.

# GLOSSARY

**abadás**—Special pants that may be part of a capoeirista's uniform.

**agility**—The ability to move quickly and lightly.

**agogô**—A set of metal bells struck to make a melodic percussion sound in the music of capoeira.

**atabaque**—The primary percussion instrument played in the roda.

**aú**—A movement similar to a cartwheel.

**batizado e troca de corda**—The ceremony to initiate new students to capoeira, and to present students with the next level of cord in capoeira regional.

**berimbau**—The primary instrument used in the roda.

**capoeirista**—A person who practices capoeira.

**cardiovascular exercise**—Exercise that promotes heart and lung health.

**caxixí**—The woven basket that some berimbau players hold to create a rattle sound.

**esquiva**—A common maneuver used in capoeira to dodge or escape an attack.

**feint**—A type of movement made to confuse an opponent.

**ginga**—A rocking motion that is the basis of movement in capoeira.

**jogo**—The game or match of capoeira.

**mestre**—A master of capoeira.

**negativa**—A movement in capoeira that can either be a dodge of an attack, or can be used to initiate an attack.

**roda**—The circle made by a group of capoeiristas.

**rolê**—A spinning movement used to move over a distance in capoeira.

**self-confidence**—Feeling a sense of confidence in oneself and in one's abilities.

**stamina**—The ability to continue exercise or movement for a long period of time.

**sweeps**—Gliding movements of the arms or legs.

FIND OUT MORE

BOOKS

Ancona, George. *Capoeira: Game! Dance! Martial Art!* New York: Lee & Low Books, 2007.

Gifford, Clive. *Martial Arts Legends.* New York: Crabtree Publishing Company, 2009.

Ollhoff, Jim. *Martial Arts around the Globe.* Edina, MN: ABDO Publishing Company, 2008.

WEBSITES

Athletes for Education Foundation: Capoeira Kids
http://www.afefoundation.org/mindinho-capoeira-kids.html

Capoeira: Discovery Channel Martial Arts
http://www.yourdiscovery.com/martialarts/americas/capoeira/index.shtml

Time for Kids: Brazil
http://www.timeforkids.com/TFK/kids/specials/articles/0,28285,190784,00.html

# INDEX

Page numbers in **boldface** are illustrations.

## ABOUT THE AUTHOR

Johannah Haney is a freelance writer in Boston. She has written several books for young readers for Marshall Cavendish about endangered species, pets, and health.